Little Guides to
Great Lives

MARIE CURIE

LAURENCE KING

Published in 2018
by Laurence King Publishing Ltd
361–373 City Road
London EC1V 1LR
United Kingdom
Tel: +44 20 7841 6900
Fax: +44 20 7841 6910
E-mail: enquiries@laurenceking.com
www.laurenceking.com

Illustrations © 2018 Anke Weckmann

A catalog record for this book is available
from the British Library

ISBN: 978-1-78627-153-2

Commissioning Editor: Chloë Pursey
Editor: Katherine Pitt
Design: Charlotte Bolton

Printed in China

Other *Little Guides to Great Lives*:
Charles Darwin
Amelia Earhart
Frida Kahlo
Leonardo da Vinci
Nelson Mandela

Little Guides to
Great Lives

MARIE
CURIE

Written by
Isabel Thomas

Illustrations by
Anke Weckmann

Laurence King Publishing

What made Marie Curie one of the world's most famous scientists? There are clues in the way she spoke about science:

I am among those who think that science has great beauty.

A scientist in his laboratory is not only a technician: he is also a child placed before natural phenomena which delight him like a fairy tale.

The story of Marie's life is like a fairy tale—with happy and sad times, struggles, and triumphs. Watch out for a metal called <u>radium</u> that is both the hero and the villain.

Marie was born in Warsaw, Poland. She was the youngest of FIVE brothers and sisters.

Dr. Władysław Skłodowski
Maths and <u>physics</u> teacher

Bronisława Skłodowska
Headteacher

Zosia

Joseph

Bronia

Hela

Later, I changed my name to "Marie"

Maria
Born 7 November 1867

At this time, part of Poland
—including Warsaw—was
under Russian control.

The Russians wanted us to
forget about being Polish and live
exactly like they did. But we secretly
helped our children to learn our
language and culture.

All the children loved learning, but Marie was the
brainiest. One day, Bronia was getting cross because
she couldn't read a sentence. Marie peered over her
shoulder and read the whole thing out loud. Her parents
were shocked—no one had taught Marie to read yet!

When Marie was nine, her sister Zosia died of typhus. Less than two years later, Marie's mother died of tuberculosis. For a long time, Marie was desperately sad, and her father was becoming poorer and poorer.

When it was time for Marie to start secondary school, she didn't know what to feel. She LOVED learning, but the schools were run by the Russian government and very strict.

Marie had a personality to match her curly, wild hair.

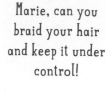

Marie, can you braid your hair and keep it under control!

Happily, Marie had a best
friend to help her cope.

She loved going back to
Kazia's grand home for lemonade
and chocolate ice cream!

Marie passed all her exams a year early, and enjoyed a year in the countryside, away from books and studying.

She returned to Warsaw when she was 16, happier than before but with a big worry.

Her brother Joseph had started training to be a doctor, but girls in Russian Poland weren't allowed to go to university. Marie only had three options...

What next?

1.
Get a job as a teacher
(like Mother)

2.
Get married
(but I'm much too young!)

3.
Go to university in a different
country (but Father is too
poor to afford it)

Then she received a very special invitation...

A secret location

Girls should have the same opportunities
as boys, so I am setting up a secret
university. We will meet for two
hours every week, for lessons from
top scientists, thinkers, and historians.
Girls too poor to pay can still
come along.

We must keep this secret from the
Russian police, so please destroy
this letter.

By 1889, 1000 girls were enrolled in Warsaw's "floating university." Marie and her sister Bronia loved learning and desperately wanted to continue their studies abroad —but it was too expensive.

So Marie came up with a plan: she would find work as a teacher, and save enough money to send Bronia to Paris. Then, once Bronia had become a doctor, Marie would join her.

Eighteen-year-old Marie became a governess and moved into the family's large, beautiful house. The plan worked—she soon saved enough money to send Bronia to Paris—but Marie was bored and frustrated...

"When will it be MY turn to go to university?"

AT LAST the letter she was waiting for arrived. Marie was invited to live with Bronia and her new husband in Paris.

Marie moved to France in 1891, bringing everything she owned—even her mattress! She enrolled in the world-famous Sorbonne University to study her favorite subjects: physics and mathematics.

Marie worked so hard she often forgot to eat (and could barely afford food anyway)...

...But I was SO HAPPY!

In 1894, she met Pierre Curie—a brilliant scientist working at the Sorbonne. A year later, they were married.

As Marie and Pierre cycled off on honeymoon, they had no idea that they were about to change the world.

Marie was ready to begin her <u>doctorate</u>—her first piece of research as a scientist. Before scientists can look for answers, they need... Questions!

Marie began reading and making notes about all the latest discoveries in physics and <u>chemistry</u> to find out what was new and exciting.

The first hang-glider flights

Electrical generator invented

Radio waves used for communication

<u>X-rays</u> discovered

Mysterious <u>uranium</u> rays

* URANIUM!!! *

In 1896 scientists were very excited about X-rays—mysterious, invisible beams that could pass through solid objects and take amazing photographs of bones!

So when scientist Henri Becquerel noticed that a metal called uranium also gave out invisible rays, no one paid much attention. X-rays were much stronger after all. But Marie was intrigued...

I wonder if any other materials also give out these rays?

"The question was entirely new and, even better, nobody else had written about it."

Marie decided to find out. She began by testing all the underlined elements. These are the building blocks of everything on Earth, and they had all been listed in a handy chart called the periodic table.

No luck! But Marie didn't give up.

She tested minerals next—those lumps of rock displayed at natural history museums. Other scientists weren't doing this. After all, minerals were just different mixtures of the elements Marie had already tested.

She even tested <u>pitchblende</u>, the heavy, black rock that contained small amounts of uranium.

And got a huge surprise...

Marie was puzzled. Working with Pierre, she tested the pitchblende again and again to make sure. Then she found a second mineral that gave out these invisible rays—and this one had no uranium in it.

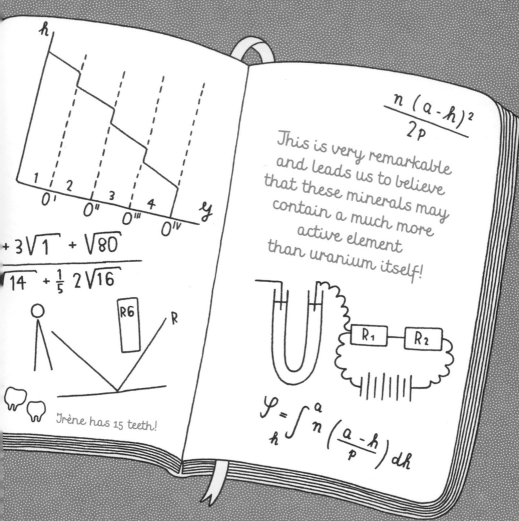

$$\frac{n(a-h)^2}{2p}$$

This is very remarkable and leads us to believe that these minerals may contain a much more active element than uranium itself!

$$+3\sqrt{1} + \sqrt{80}$$
$$\overline{14 + \frac{1}{5} \, 2\sqrt{16}}$$

Irène has 15 teeth!

$$\mathcal{S} = \int_h^a n\left(\frac{a-h}{p}\right) dh$$

Scientists love unexpected discoveries and new questions, so Marie was very excited.

But other scientists weren't so sure.

EXCITING THING #1:
There must be a BRAND NEW ELEMENT hidden in the pitchblende! It gave out rays so strong, they could pass through ANYTHING except a thick sheet of lead.

EXCITING THING #2:
The rays must be caused by something deep inside the <u>atoms</u> that we don't know about!

I made 14 pots of very good jam.

Irène says "Gogli, gogli, go."

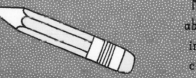

Marie also wrote small notes about her baby daughter Irène in her journals, right next to complex scientific equations.

The only way to prove it once and for all was to extract the mystery element from the pitchblende. No one could argue that an element didn't exist if they were holding it in their hands!

Pierre gave up his own research and joined Marie in her mission. It was not going to be easy.

REASONS WE SHOULDN'T

No money
(Pierre can't get a professor job at the Sorbonne, and is still a badly paid teacher)

Full-time jobs as teachers, so we'll have to work at night

No laboratory, just a few wooden tables in a freezing room!

A baby (Irène) to look after

No help

✳ REASONS WE SHOULD ✳

We are TOO EXCITED to stop!

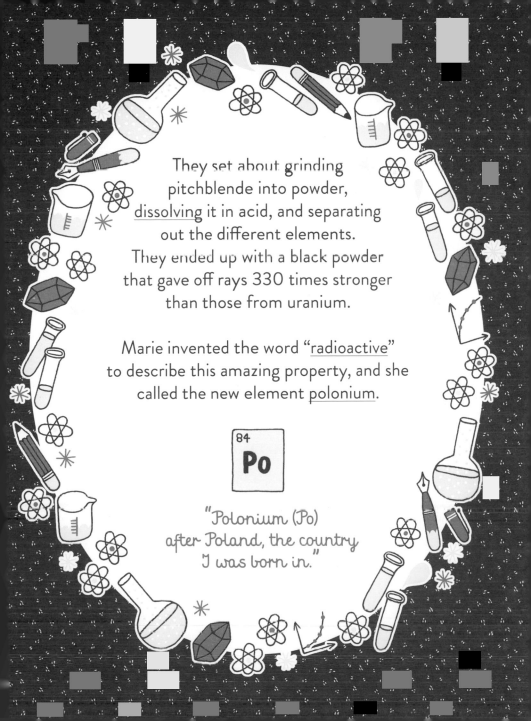

They set about grinding
pitchblende into powder,
<u>dissolving</u> it in acid, and separating
out the different elements.
They ended up with a black powder
that gave off rays 330 times stronger
than those from uranium.

Marie invented the word "<u>radioactive</u>"
to describe this amazing property, and she
called the new element <u>polonium</u>.

84
Po

"Polonium (Po)
after Poland, the country
I was born in."

Marie and Pierre noticed that the liquid left behind after extracting polonium and uranium from pitchblende was still very radioactive.

This was a clue that pitchblende contained a tiny amount of a SECOND new element—much more radioactive than polonium and uranium!

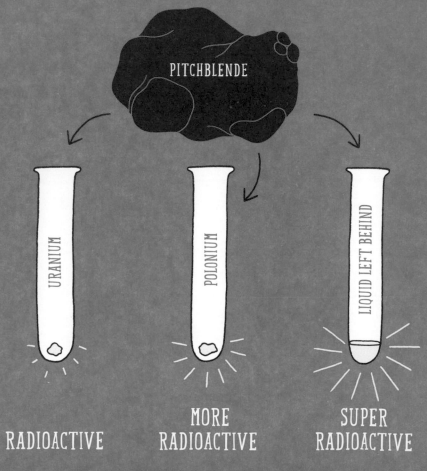

PITCHBLENDE

URANIUM

POLONIUM

LIQUID LEFT BEHIND

RADIOACTIVE

MORE RADIOACTIVE

SUPER RADIOACTIVE

They announced the discovery in 1898, and called the new element "radium."

LE JOURNAL

Paris

1898

NEW ELEMENT DISCOVERED

RADIUM: FROM THE LATIN WORD RADIUS, MEANING "RAY"

While Pierre studied the properties of the rays themselves, Marie decided to extract this new metal. To do this, she would need more pitchblende. LOTS more pitchblende.

Pitchblende was expensive and Marie and Pierre were poor. So Marie bought the waste materials from a factory that took uranium out of pitchblende.

Little did the factory know, this leftover dust contained something even more precious than uranium!

Marie began to work with the pitchblende to extract the tiny particles of hidden radium. It was a bit like boiling away water to leave salt behind, but much, much harder!

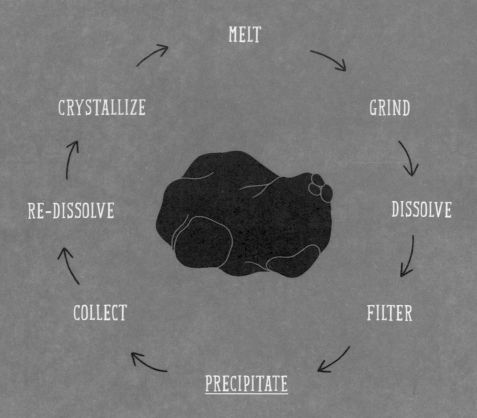

MELT

CRYSTALLIZE

GRIND

RE-DISSOLVE

DISSOLVE

COLLECT

FILTER

PRECIPITATE

It was hard work to carry the containers, to pour off the liquids, and to stir the boiling material in a cast-iron basin for hours at a time—and then have to do it all over again!

They worked in a rickety shed with a sticky
tar floor, and a broken glass roof that let
heat out and rain in.

Marie and Pierre began to feel sick
and exhausted. They had no idea that
<u>radiation</u> was dangerous.

Marie got closer and closer to her goal, extracting liquids so radioactive that they glowed.

"One of our pleasures was to enter our workshop at night; then, all around us, we would see

minous silhouettes of the beakers and capsules that contained our "products."

It took THREE YEARS, but in 1902 Marie finally extracted
one milligram of radium from ten tons of pitchblende!

Marie was awarded her doctorate of physics in June 1903 —the first woman in Europe to get this qualification.

In the same year, Marie, Pierre, and Henri Becquerel shared the world's top science award—the Nobel Prize in Physics—for their work on radioactivity.

They were now science superstars.

·NOBEL· PRIZE· ·IN· ·PHYSICS·

MARIE CURIE
MCMIII

"Irène adores her new big penny!"

Everyone wanted to know how to extract radium, and use its exciting new properties. Marie and Pierre could have become rich by charging scientists and businesses to use their method.

Instead, they shared their knowledge for free, so doctors could begin to use radium without delay.

Radium should belong to everyone!

Telegrams of congratulations piled up on the table. Thousands of newspaper articles were written. Everyone wanted their photograph. But Marie and Pierre didn't want to be rich or famous. They just wanted time and space to be scientists.

They had a new puzzle to solve.

Radiation is a type of energy.

Marie and Pierre knew that another type of radiation—light—was released by chemical reactions inside the Sun...

...or when a wire got very hot inside a light bulb.

But radium gave out radiation without reacting with anything, and without being heated.

Where did this mysterious energy come from?

In 1904, Marie began her first paid job in science, as Chief Assistant at the laboratory run by Pierre. They also had their second baby—a daughter called Ève.

For almost two years, Marie and Pierre worked together on the science they loved. Pierre was finally appointed a professor at the Sorbonne.

On the weekends, the family enjoyed bicycle trips to explore the countryside, wandering through woods, chasing butterflies, and collecting flowers.

They didn't know that something terrible was about to happen.

One rainy
morning in 1906,
Pierre stepped
into the road as he
walked to the lab, and
was run over by a
horse-drawn truck.

He was killed
instantly.

I enter the room. Someone says: "He is dead." Can one comprehend such words?

Pierre is dead, he who I had seen leave looking fine this morning...he is gone forever, leaving me nothing but desolation and despair.

At first, Marie felt she would never want to work again. But when she was offered the chance to stop working and be paid a pension as a widow, she refused. She became determined to complete the work they had started together.

Marie took over Pierre's teaching role, and in 1908 she became the first female professor in the history of the Sorbonne.

As well as giving lectures, she continued to run the busy laboratory, overseeing the work of other scientists.

She also wrote a huge number of important papers and books, publishing her most famous work in 1910.

TREATISE ON RADIO-ACTIVITY

971 PAGES LONG!

In 1911, Marie achieved another amazing first—a SECOND Nobel Prize, this time in Chemistry! No one in the world had won two Nobel Prizes before.

Once again, Marie's name was in every newspaper and she was chased by photographers on the street.

This time, journalists had unkind things to say. Marie had become close to another scientist, Paul Langevin, who was married to someone else. It was a scandal, and the Nobel Committee asked her not to come and collect her prize in person.

Marie did not care what other people thought, and she went anyway.

By 1914, Marie was looking forward to moving into a brand new laboratory that she had designed: the Radium Institute at the Sorbonne.

But the work was postponed. The biggest war the world had ever seen was breaking out.

Marie immediately offered to help France in any way she could. She knew lots about X-rays, so she decided to make sure that X-ray equipment was available in as many French hospitals as possible.

X-rays leave a "shadow" on photographic film.

They can travel through skin and muscle, but not through metal.

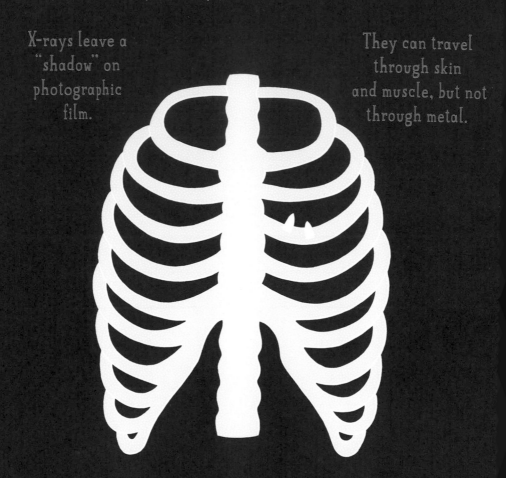

This helped doctors to spot bullets and shrapnel, and remove them before they did even more harm.

Marie was frustrated—by the time soldiers made it to hospital, it was often too late to save them. If only injuries could be diagnosed sooner, more lives could be saved.

She came up with an amazing plan: a car with built-in X-ray equipment, powered by the car's engine. It could be driven to any hospital where it was needed.

Marie didn't stop at one car. She toured Paris, asking for money, supplies, and vehicles to convert. People were pleased to help a world-famous scientist, and she soon built a fleet of mobile X-ray unit trucks known as "little Curies."

Thanks to Marie's hard work, there were:

20 MOBILE TRUCKS

200 FIXED X-RAY POSTS ESTABLISHED

150 WOMEN TRAINED AS X-RAY TECHNICIANS

Marie worked as a driver herself, X-raying casualties near the battlefields of World War I. She even trained 17-year-old Irène to run a unit on her own.

Her efforts helped to make X-ray departments a vital part of every hospital—not only during war, but in times of peace.

After the war, Marie continued her work as a scientist, teacher, and head of her laboratory at the Radium Institute. She employed many female scientists, including Irène.

It became one of the best places in the world to study radioactive substances, and the ways they could be used to treat cancer and other illnesses.

Marie was more famous than ever, and she was invited to tour the USA. Although she hated the spotlight, and the thought of the long journey by ship across the Atlantic Ocean, Marie accepted because she knew it would help her raise more money to plough into her research.

In 1921, the USA gave Marie a gift of one gram of pure radium. At the time, this was worth $100,000 —$2,000,000 in today's money. Radium was still the only source of intense radiation, so it was vital for the research in the lab. In 1929, the USA presented her with enough money to buy a second precious gram.

Many of the world's most brilliant physicists, including Albert Einstein, were now exploring the powerful forces inside atoms.

The radiation released by radium is good at killing diseased cells, but it can damage healthy cells too.

Since Marie and Pierre had discovered the element in 1898, people had been using it everywhere—not just in medical treatments, but to make glow-in-the-dark paints, teddy bears with glowing eyes, and Christmas tree lights that were supposed to be safer than candles.

In darkness,
the glow from radium
was strong enough to
read by!

But in the 1930s, people who worked closely with radium, such as factory workers who used radium paint, began to get ill, and to die. The world realized how dangerous radioactive substances really are.

Marie had suffered from radiation sickness without knowing it. Years of working with radioactive substances had damaged the cells in her bones that make new red blood cells. On 4 July 1934, Marie died, aged just 66.

Happily, she had lived to see one of her biggest dreams come true—a brand new Radium Institute in Warsaw, Poland, a center for research and the treatment of cancer. It was paid for by fundraising, and led by her sister Bronia.

MARII
SKŁODOWSKIJ CURIE
W HOŁDZIE

She also saw Irène (and husband Frédéric Joliot) produce artificial radioactivity, a discovery that won them a Nobel Prize of their own.

By turning a common metal like aluminum into a radioactive substance, we can use radioactivity without having to hunt for the rare and dangerous radioactive substances that exist in nature.

None of this would have been possible without Marie Curie's determination and dedication.

Marie Curie had all the ingredients of a great scientist:

CURIOSITY:
She never stopped looking
and ASKING QUESTIONS

CREATIVITY:
A brain that made
CONNECTIONS no one
else had made yet

RADIOLOGIE

GRIT:
The ability to KEEP GOING
when things are tough

This combination of characteristics helped her to
make discoveries that changed physics, chemistry,
and medicine forever.

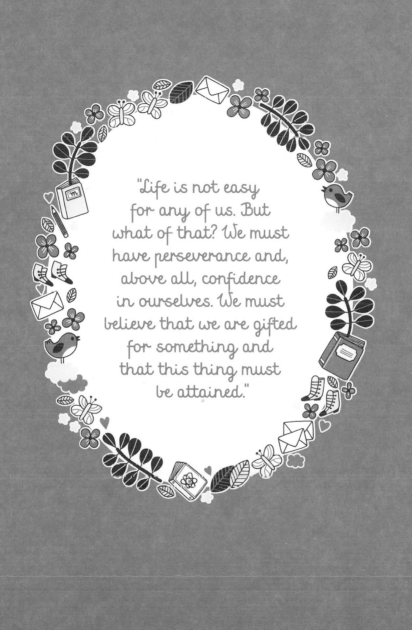

"Life is not easy
for any of us. But
what of that? We must
have perseverance and,
above all, confidence
in ourselves. We must
believe that we are gifted
for something and
that this thing must
be attained."

THE IMPACTS OF MARIE'S AMAZING DISCOVERIES

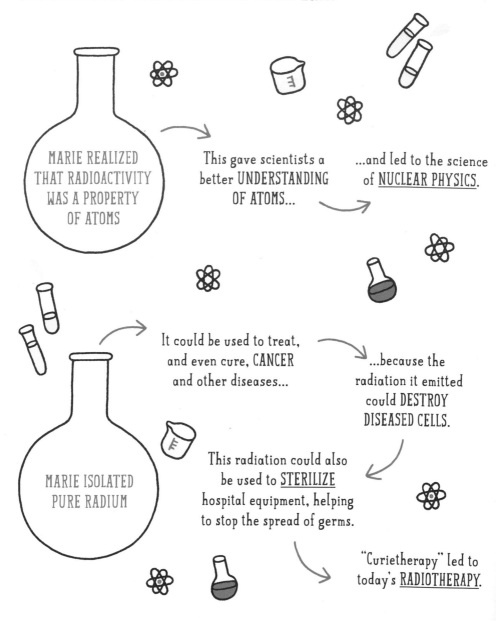

MARIE REALIZED THAT RADIOACTIVITY WAS A PROPERTY OF ATOMS

This gave scientists a better UNDERSTANDING OF ATOMS...

...and led to the science of NUCLEAR PHYSICS.

MARIE ISOLATED PURE RADIUM

It could be used to treat, and even cure, CANCER and other diseases...

...because the radiation it emitted could DESTROY DISEASED CELLS.

This radiation could also be used to STERILIZE hospital equipment, helping to stop the spread of germs.

"Curietherapy" led to today's RADIOTHERAPY.

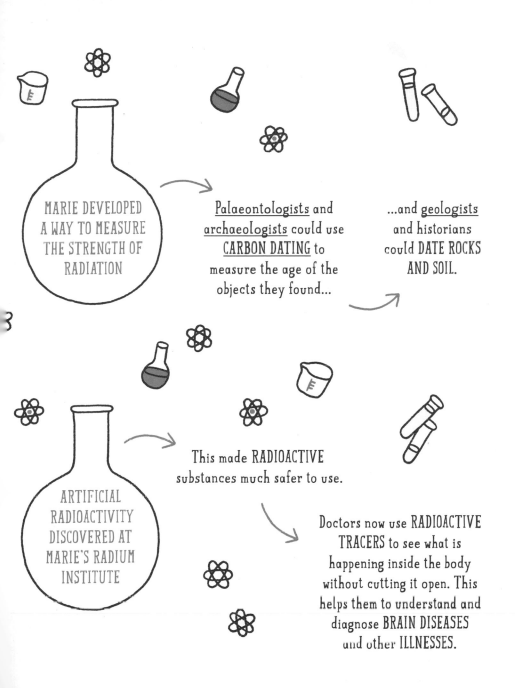

MARIE DEVELOPED A WAY TO MEASURE THE STRENGTH OF RADIATION

Palaeontologists and archaeologists could use CARBON DATING to measure the age of the objects they found...

...and geologists and historians could DATE ROCKS AND SOIL.

ARTIFICIAL RADIOACTIVITY DISCOVERED AT MARIE'S RADIUM INSTITUTE

This made RADIOACTIVE substances much safer to use.

Doctors now use RADIOACTIVE TRACERS to see what is happening inside the body without cutting it open. This helps them to understand and diagnose BRAIN DISEASES and other ILLNESSES.

TIMELINE

1867
Maria Skłodowska is born in Warsaw, Poland, on 7 November.

1880s
Maria and her sister Bronia enrol in Warsaw's "floating university."

1886
Maria becomes a governess for the Szczuki family.

1897
Marie and Pierre's daughter Irène is born.

1898
The Curies announce the discovery of two elements, radium and polonium.

1903
Marie becomes the first woman in Europe to graduate with a doctorate in physics.

That same year, Marie and Pierre are awarded a joint Nobel Prize in Physics.

1910
Treatise on Radioactivity is published.

1911
Marie receives a second Nobel Prize, this time in Chemistry. She is still the only woman to be awarded two Nobel Prizes.

1914
Marie moves into the Radium Institute at the Sorbonne...

1930s
People begin to discover the harmful effects of radiation.

1932
The Radium Institute opens in Warsaw, Poland.

1934
On 4 July, Marie dies at the age of 66 from radiation sickness.

1891
Marie moves to France to study physics and mathematics at the Sorbonne in Paris. She changes her name to "Marie."

1895
Marie and Pierre Curie get married.

1896
Henri Becquerel discovers the invisible rays emitted by uranium. This discovery spurs on Marie's own research.

1904
Marie becomes Chief Assistant at Pierre's laboratory —her first paid job in science!

Marie and Pierre's second daughter, Ève, is born. 💜

1906
Pierre is killed in a traffic accident.

1908
Marie becomes a Professor of Physics at the Sorbonne, making her the first female professor in the university's history.

1914
...but her work is interrupted by World War I. Eager to help wounded soldiers, she creates a fleet of "petite Curie" X-ray trucks.

1918
After the war, Marie continues to research radioactive substances at the Radium Institute.

1921
Marie visits the USA to raise money for her research.

Today
Radiation therapy remains a vital part of cancer treatment.

Marie's notebooks are still so radioactive that they have to be kept in special lead-lined boxes!

Marie Curie

GLOSSARY

archaeology – the study of human history through the excavation (digging up) of important sites. The objects archaeologists find contain clues about the people who used to live there, sometimes thousands of years ago.

atom – a chemical element's smallest part, made up of <u>electrons</u>, <u>protons</u>, and <u>neutrons</u>. These are known as subatomic particles.

carbon dating – determining an object's age by measuring the level of radioactive carbon it contains. This can be done because carbon loses neutrons at a regular rate.

chemistry – the study of matter (things such as atoms, gases, and elements) and how they interact with each other.

dissolve – to incorporate a solid substance into a liquid so it forms a solution. You can dissolve sugar in your tea, for example.

doctorate – the highest degree awarded by universities.

electron – a tiny particle within an atom that contains a negative electrical charge. On its own, an atom is electrically neutral, so when it gains an electron it becomes negatively charged, and when it loses an electron it becomes positively charged.

element – a substance that cannot be chemically changed or broken down into a simpler substance. There are 92 naturally occurring elements, such as aluminum, gold, and helium; 26 more have been created in laboratories, making 118 elements in total.

geology – the study, through the examination of rocks and soil, of the Earth's structure and how it changes over time.

Nobel Prize – a set of prizes awarded each year for outstanding work in areas such as science, medicine, and literature. The prize was started by the Swedish inventor Alfred Nobel in 1895.

nuclear physics – the study of atoms' protons and neutrons.

neutron – a subatomic particle found within the nuclei (center) of all atoms, except hydrogen's atom. Neutrons contain no electrical charge.

palaeontology – the study of bones and fossils that have been preserved in rock or soil for thousands, sometimes millions, of years.

periodic table – a list of the 118 chemical elements that have been discovered (so far...), in order of atomic number. Chemicals with similar properties, such as metals, are grouped together.

physics – the study of matter and energy, and how these forces interact.

pitchblende – a black mineral that contains radium.

polonium – a radioactive metallic element with the symbol Po and atomic number 84. Polonium is created by decaying uranium.

precipitate – to create an insoluble solid (something that cannot be dissolved) from a liquid solution.

proton – a subatomic particle found within an atom's nucleus. Protons have a positive electrical charge that's equal to an electron's negative charge. A chemical element's atomic number, which decides its place in the periodic table, is based on the number of protons within its atom.

radiation – a type of energy that emits rays, waves, or particles.

radio wave – a type of electromagnetic radiation, commonly used to transmit radio and television signals.

radioactive – having or producing radiation. Radiation is measured in units called "curies," named after Marie and Pierre.

radiotherapy – the treatment of diseases using radiation.

radium – a metallic chemical element with the symbol Ra and atomic number 88. Radium is very radioactive and is found in pitchblende.

sterilize – to remove all the germs and bacteria from an object or substance.

uranium – a chemical element with the symbol U and atomic number 92. It is a highly radioactive, silvery-white metal.

X-ray – an electromagnetic wave that can pass through certain solid materials, such as skin and muscle, and leaves a shadow on photographic paper.

INDEX

CREDITS

Photograph of Marie Curie on page 61 courtesy of the Library of Congress